8/22

Bert and I

and Other Stories
from Down East

Bert and I

and Other Stories
from Down East

*by Marshall Dodge
and Robert Bryan*

Illustrations by Mark Andres

Bert and I, Inc. / Rowley MA
with
Down East Books / Camden, ME

Printed and bound at Versa Press, East Peoria, IL
5   4   3   2   1

Down East Books   Bert and I, Inc
P.O. Box 679   P.O. Box 92
Camden, ME 04843   Rowley, MA 01960
Book orders: 800-685-7962

ISBN: 0-89272-560-5

Library of Congress Control Number: 2001097007

Bert and I was set in Baskerville, Hiroshige, and Monotype Corsiva
to a design by Wayne Hammond, based on original layouts by
Mark Andres.

Introduction

It is impossible to truly know Maine without understanding the enduring appeal of *Bert and I*. For within the imaginary psyches of Marshall Dodge's and Robert Bryan's brilliantly sardonic characters resides an indelible part of Maine that hasn't been tainted or altered by the onrushing vacuous sprawl of modern popular culture.

Internationally, MTV may be the most visible symbol of a new generation's desire to "rock the house," but the stories of our boys from Down East Maine can still bring the house down with laughter.

What is it that has endeared us to these stories? What is it about them that causes people to rush to listen to them or read them again and again and to still laugh out loud uncontrollably, even when they get to a punch line they can already recite from memory?

The secret to *Bert and I*'s timeless appeal, of course, lies in the Maine mystique. You see, *Bert and I* was never intended to be a parody of Maine life but rather a celebration of it.

The essence of a place like Maine is engendered by a subtle interplay of the land, the sea, and the people. The story of one cannot be told without telling the tales of the others. And while story-telling Down East has long—on its face—been about places and things, in reality its essence is about the spirit of the people and their resolute way of life—the way they've surmounted obstacles at once economic, physical, and spiritual with pluck, aplomb, a dash of dry fatalism; but always with a wonderful sense of humor concerning the unpredictable yet inevitable twists and tribulations of life. In this respect Maine's spirit, while not necessarily unique, is unrivaled.

Maine humor is readily recognizable. Yet unlike other humor genres, where you can just insert the target of your choice (dumb blondes, travelling salesmen, etc.), Maine jokes just don't work very well if you substitute another place. Who, for instance, could explain what Connecticut humor is? Or who, for that matter, can recite a good Nebraska joke?

The secret, though, is quite simple. The laughs in Maine humor, in marked contrast to other forms of comedy, including slapstick and the expletive-filled monologues of sarcastic club comedians, come at no one else's expense. No one is laughing at anybody else. Everyone is laughing together.

The fact that the creators of *Bert and I* were not natives often comes as a surprise to people. But the fact that they possessed the clarity of thought to discern the essence of the state and the talent to convey it to the rest of us testifies mightily to their affection for Maine.

That affection is not something you can announce. It can only be proved by deed as well as by word over time. In Maine, new arrivals have to wait to be drawn in; you can't push or bull your way to the forefront. Those who try often discover the net effect is just the opposite.

Over the centuries many people who have come to Maine from away have enjoyed a disproportionate economic advantage. In that sense there have been few pieces of land, industry, or business, and few beautiful places that have been beyond the reach of those with considerable means. The one thing, though, that has always remained beyond the reach of money is acceptance. And, much like any great treasure, it is not parcelled out quickly; only after due deliberation and quiet examination.

The fact that the *Bert and I* stories over the years have retained a timeless appeal proves they pass this test and bear, for want of a better metaphor, the Down East Maine "Good Housekeeping Seal of Approval."

I have had the great fortune in my life of meeting the principals of *Bert and I* in person, though not both at the same time.

Years ago, while covering a story about land conservation Down East, I got to spend an afternoon with Bob Bryan flying in his float plane to his beloved Tunk Lake east of Ellsworth.

His indomitable spirit and love of northern lands and their peoples, which prompted him to found the Quebec-Labrador Foundation, is evident in every fiber of his being. The same intuition and powers of observation he brought to the creation of *Bert and I* continue to serve him well today.

I had a chance to spend an evening listening to the late Marshall Dodge in Bar Harbor many, many years ago. He was a talented speaker with a soft-spoken delivery style that prompted listeners to lean in at just the right moment for him to deliver the punch line.

On the evening I saw him, Mr. Dodge did not spend as much time reprising the familiar Maine stories as he did talking about the differences between Eastern and Western humor. He explained that the tellers of tall tales out West approached their craft as braggarts, laughing at the listeners for believing such whopping lies.

Eastern humor, noted Mr. Dodge, gets the listeners to laugh at themselves for not seeing the homespun and often painfully obvious twist which inevitably comes at the end of the story. Eastern humor, Down East humor to be exact, will always triumph, he noted, because when everybody laughs, everybody wins.

Mr. Dodge offered a short and clear comparison pitting a tall-tale-telling Texas rancher against an understated Maine farmer. In a wonderful drawl, he said "Yep. My ranch in Texas goes on for miles. It is so big, it takes me four days to drive around it in my car."

Dodge then shifted to his deliberate yet never overdone Down East accent, snapped the suspenders on an imaginary pair of overalls, and replied, "Ayuh, back on my fahrm in Maine we gotta cah just like that."

One popular rock and roll video on MTV in recent years featured the song "The Boys are Back in Town." With the return of *Bert and I* in this book and the re-release of the original recordings, there will be some who'll observe that it's nice our boys are back. But *Bert and I* stories have always been a unique part of that which engenders the broader spirit of all things Maine. And they always will be.

Earl Brechlin
Bar Harbor
October, 2001

Foreword

"It don't hardly seem possible" that twenty-three years
have passed since two audacious Yale students set out to
produce a phonograph record of Down East stories, under
the name "Bert and I." But the years have passed as
certainly as the recording has flourished.

Those two young men are now twenty-three years older.
Marshall Dodge lives in Maine and travels the nation
interpreting his neighbors to their remote cousins, and
gives to the arts and humanities of his adopted state at
least as much as he takes. Bob Bryan lives in Ipswich,
Massachusetts, and devotes his limitless energies to the
Quebec-Labrador Foundation, no doubt finding in the
people of that region many of the qualities he so admires
in New England Yankees.

But if Dodge and Bryan have done both good and well in
the intervening years, the durability of "Bert and I" (and its
sequels) has been at least as remarkable. The record album
has sustained its appeal over a span of years that included
wars and Watergate, bear markets and bare bosoms. It has
outlasted the service of six Presidents of the United States.
Born of the Silent Generation, "Bert and I" survived even
the SDS.

"Bert and I" is not in any other way to be compared with
the Bible; but, apart from the Good Book, it's hard to imagine
that any other publication or platter has worn so well during
these two decades. Best sellers have hopped past us like so

many hares, while the genial tortoise, "Bert and I" astride, has kept plugging right along.

It all seems to suggest that there is something about the appeal of plain people, sympathetically caricatured, that is well nigh universal. "Bert and I" seem in some ways descendants of Tom and Huck and Jim. They are representatives of an endangered regionalism, talking reminders of what is at stake when a society trades its stability for mobility. It may be nothing more than a romantic urge to cling to older times, older ways, that makes listeners and readers chuckle with warmth and affection, as the Downeaster outsmarts the city slicker. But even if that's all it is, it's a reminder of the price we pay for progress; and the creators of "Bert and I" deserve to be acknowledged as cultural conservationists.

Twenty-three years ago, in writing the liner notes for the first edition of "Bert and I," I marvelled at the sound effects created by Dodge and Bryan: the sound of fog horns, the Bangor Packet, and seemingly unmuffled sports cars. In enjoying its printed form, of course, the reader will have to supply those effects. But the accumulated listenership of twenty years will only have to close its eyes for an instant to recall those unforgettable sounds.

It is a new marvel that "Bert and I" are now joined by Mark Andres. If the sounds and soft accents of the phonograph record are lost, they are admirably, indeed impressively, replaced by Mr. Andres' illustrations. Just as the Down East accent seems to take the harshness out of everyday life in New England, so do Mark Andres' soft pencilled lines take the edge from the chiseled and grizzled faces of his subjects. Thanks to him, we haven't lost the sounds, but gained the sights. What might have been nothing more than a libretto has become—thanks to these illustrations—a genuine new creation.

It is a pleasure, then, to welcome "Bert and I" to what has become known, in their lifetime, as the "print media." The pleasure is distinct, because in a world that has skidded and slipped into jargon (and even greater sins), it's nice to welcome a good old-fashioned *book* filled with images, verbal and pictorial, that reflects timeless and enduring values that Marshall and Bob and Mark and Bert and yes, I, so admire.

HOMER D. BABBIDGE, JR.

Hartford, April 1981

Contents

Bert and I

Bert and I come down to the dock about
six o'clock in the early mornin'.

Bert went into the baitshack to get some chum, and I went out on the dock to start up the *Bluebird*. It was cold as I stepped into the cockpit to loosen her up with a few turns.

Sa * ha.

Sa * ha.

SA

* ha

* ha.

You could hear it were cold, so I advanced the spark and give it more choke and cranked her up in earnest.

SAHA. SAHA.
SABAM. SABAM.

BAM TICKA BAM TICKA TICKA

BAM BAM
BAM BAM

Well, I got it hummin'.

TICKA

Bert come out on the dock with the chum.

"Throw it aboard, Bert."
Bert threw it aboard.
"Cast off the bow, Bert."

Bert cast off the bow, he cast off the stern, loosed the springer, hopped aboard, gave the dock a shove with the gaff, and the *Bluebird* slithered out into harbor.

BAM ticka ticka ticka BAM BAM ticka BAM

That old make-and-break Knox Marine one-lunger engine may sound rough-runnin' to your ears, but if it fired once every twelve strokes, it was runnin' smooth. The flywheel was enough to carry it in between explosions.

We hit nun number two about on schedule, when I sniffed a cold breeze comin' in off the ocean, heavy with humdidy.

It weren't long before old Greasy Frog light started
in a-phomphin'.

Pretty soon we were locked in a dungeon of fog.

I couldn't see Bert and he couldn't see me. I told Bert to cut engine so's we could listen for the Bangor Packet about due through at that time.

"Cut engine, Bert."

BAM ticka ticka BAM ticka   ticka   ticka

                       tic ka   tic ka

                                       cough *

                ticka   BAM *cough* * *cough* *

                                        ticka *cough* *

                       ticka *cough* *

Sa * ah ah *ha* ah *ha* ah *haaaaaaaaaaaaaaaaaa*

                                        Bert cut engine.

OOOOOOOOOOOOOOOOFFFFFFFFF

That were the hum of the Bangor Packet, about a half mile
to starboard.
"Give a blast of the horn, Bert."

Aaaaaaaaaaaaghhhhhhh!

Bert gave a blast of the horn.

OOOOOOOOOOOOOOOOFFFFFFFFF

That were the Packet, about a quarter mile to starboard.
"Give it another one, Bert."

"That were a good 'un, Bert."

RSHLE
WHIRSHLE

But it weren't good enough,
for out of the fog about a hundred
yards to starboard come the Bangor Packet,
bearin' down at a full ten knots, straight for
the *Bluebird*.

SCROINCH!!

The Bangor Packet smuck the *Bluebird* about midships and drove on through her like green corn goes through the new maid.

The water rose up over our necks before we decided to swim for it. I dove down three fathom or so, so as to avoid the two whirrin' propellors of the Bangor Packet as she went o'er top.

I come up t'other side and cried out, "Bert, Bert, are you there?"

There weren't no answer, so I thrashed about in the water 'til I hit upon a hard object about a foot or so beneath the surface. I grabbed a-hold, pulled it up, and it were Bert, and he were spoilin' full of water.

I gave him a good squeeze and got most of the water out of him. I just held his nose above the waves as best I could 'til by some stroke of luck we fetched onto a bell buoy.

I clumb atop it, pulled Bert up beside me, emptied him out complete, and we were near dried out by the time the fishin' smack come along, picked us up, and brought us back to Kennebunkport, Maine.

Now if you're ever down East and want to go a-fishin', you have a standin' invitation to ride on the *Bluebird* II with Bert and I.

Kenneth Fowler
Goes Hunting

Kenneth Fowler had had an awful season. Everything he
planted had been eaten by blackbirds just as soon as he
scattered the seed. Fire had destroyed his blueberry ground
at rakin' time, and termites had ate up his icehouse. On top
of that, a stray cat had drowned in his well.

By October he decided he'd better stock up on food for the winter. After loadin' his gun, the one with the side-by-side barrels, he headed into the woods to find some game.

All day long he walked without firin' a shot. He was all set to quit about sundown when he spied a fox about twenty yards distance. Takin' careful aim, he almost squeezed the trigger when he saw another fox about five feet from the first.

He aimed somewhere in between and pulled the trigger.

The shot hit a rock, split in two, and killed both foxes.
The kick from the gun knocked Kenneth into the stream
behind, and when he come to, his right hand was on a
beaver's tail, his left hand was on an otter's head, and his
trouser pockets were so full of trout that a button popped
off his fly and killed a partridge.

Albert's Moose

Albert Tyler was snoozin' on his porch one mornin' when he was rudely awakened by a moose sniffin' around amongst his parsnips.

Quick as a wink, Albert had his gun off the wall and shot the moose in the hind leg, just to wound him so he wouldn't get away. The moose flopped over on his side and Albert dragged him into the barn and bedded him down for the night with hay and water—after cleanin' the moose's wound, of course.

In two days' time, Albert had the barn painted a bright red with white letterin' on the side so everyone could read it.

In a week's time, Albert's place looked more like a fair
than a farm.

A fellow come through with his family and paid fifteen cents
to see the moose. Albert took one look at the family and said,

"Take your money, mister; I don't want it. It's worth a good deal more for my moose to see your family than it can be for your family to see my moose."

The Body in the Kelp

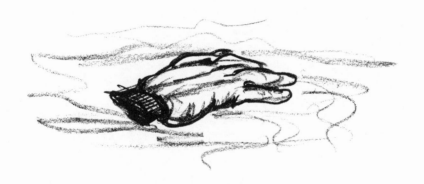

Bert and I were clammin' in the flats one Sunday and saw
a body floatin' in the kelp offshore. We figgered it might be
Old Tom who tended light out on the point. We went out
there and knocked on his door.

"You there, Tom?"

"Darn right I'm here. What can I do for you?"

"When we were clammin' this mornin', come across a body in the kelp. Thought it might have been you."

"Wearin' a red shirt?"
"Yessir. Red shirt."
"Blue trousers?"
"They were blue trousers."
"Rubber boots?"
"Ayup. Rubber boots."
"Were they high boots or low?"
"They were low boots."
"You sure they weren't high boots
turned down low?"
"Come to think of it, that's just what
they were, high boots turned down low."

"Oh well, then. T'weren't me."

Chester Coombs' Firstborn

My wife just give birth to a baby boy. She says he's some
cunnin'. But you could get me a sharp knife and a soft piece
of white pine, and I could whittle you a better-lookin' baby
than the one I got.

Harry Startles Wiscasset

Harry Whitfield bought his wife, Margaret, a truck camper
for their twentieth weddin' anniversary. He knew she would
be so tickled that she would do all the drivin', and on the
long trips, he could sleep in the back.

One Saturday night they were comin' up the long hill
through Wiscasset when Margaret stalled the camper.
She let the clutch out too fast and started up with a jerk.
Harry, who was just steppin' into his pajama bottoms
in the back, lurched up against the rear door, burst it
open, and landed spread-eagle on the center line of
Main Street.

Miss Rhoda Beale, the librarian, who was in the car behind Harry, drove onto the sidewalk and scooped the game warden on top of her hood. Traffic backed up in both directions as far as the eye could see.

Margaret, meanwhile, was halfway to Bath, none the wiser.

A crowd gathered around Harry to see what he would do next. Harry hugged the tarmac like a turtle, and cranin' his neck, spied the roof of a telephone booth over the heads of the onlookers. He made a dash for it, got inside, and slammed the door shut, only to realize it was a glass booth and he had just turned on the light.

Sergeant Orrin Wormwood pulled up his patrol car to see what all the commotion was about. He figgered Harry to be one of them streakers from Harvard. He put the cuffs on Harry and drove him up to the Lincoln County jail for observation.

Next mornin', Harry got sprung.
Margaret was waitin' for him at
the front gate, but Harry walked
right past her in a huff.

"Next time, Maggie," he said, "let the clutch out slow."

The Lighter-than-
Air Balloon

I was a spectator up to the Skowhegan fair last summer. They had stock car racin', divin' from the high platform, and teams of horses pullin' against each other. Every summer they've got a feature attraction. Years ago they had William Jennings Bryan up to regive his "Cross of Gold" speech.

This year the feature was the releasin' of a lighter-than-air balloon at twelve o'clock on the last day of the fair. Howard Perkins and I won the raffle to take her up. After a few words of instruction, we climbed into the gondola, cut the moorin' lines, and we were out of sight of land in about four minutes.

The wind carried us over the ocean in an hour and then veered north to carry us back over land.

We let some of the gas out and come down to see where we were. Saw a farmer plowin' in a field, so I cried out, "WHERE ARE WE?"

"You're in a balloon, you damn' fools."

Gagnon, World Champion Stove-Builder

Oui, I am Gagnon, world champion stove-builder, me.
I cannot afford a store-bought stove, so I take some oil
drums I find in the woods and weld and solder them
together. I have friends who come into my cabin and
laugh at my stove. "Why do you have the draft hole come
in at the top and the stove pipe in the bottom, Gagnon?"
they ask. "'Cause it make for one heck of a draft," I answer.
"You better stand back when that stove starts up," I say,
"'cause it is going to have one heck of a draft."

Then I go off to the woodshed to get me some hard wood that burns real slow and easy. A roaring sound comes out of my cabin. "Who puts soft wood in my stove and starts her up? She is going too strong!" I shout.

I have a hard time to get back inside the cabin. I have to grip the sides of the door frame because of the draft from the stove. My friends are digging their teeth and fingernails right into the cabin walls, and their legs flap in the air.

There is a clatter. The lid-lifter, the stoker, and the shovel are sucked in through the draft hole and rattle up the chimney. Then the stove lifts off the cabin floor and hits the beams of the roof.

Just when I think it will go through the shingles, there
is a terrible grinding noise and the cabin lifts off her
foundations.

I know right there I have me a stove with one
heck of a draft.

I jump up on a chair quick, and with great presence of mind turn the damper handle easy and lower the cabin back to its foundations. Slowly I turn the handle more and lower the stove back to the floor.

My friend Maurice says, "You know, Gagnon, you should have put a governor on that stove and this would not have happen."

"Governor!" I holler. "You put soft wood in that stove, Maurice, and not even the President of the United States will be able to hold it down."

The Liar

"What do you think of that man out your way? Would you call him an honest man or a liar?"

"Well, I wouldn't go so far as to call him a liar, but I heard tell by thems as knows that when he wants his cows to come in from pasture, he's got to get somebody else to call 'em."

Camden Pierce Goes
to New York City

Camden Pierce, who lives out to Mechanics Falls, was
rockin' in his parlor one afternoon, listenin' to the radio,
when the telephone started in a-janglin'.

He picked it up. It was the radio station callin'.
"Hello, this Camden Pierce?"
He said, "Yessir."
"Well, what's the name of that tune we're playin'?"
Camden knew it: "Battle Hymn of the Republic."
They said, "You got it. Besides that, you just won a
two-week's trip to New York City."

Of course, Camden had never been out of the state —
never even been to Bangor, except once. That was the
time the bull moose wandered into town and was chased
into the hardware store by the schoolchildren.

Camden left for New York, and two weeks later was back.
Mayor Johnson thought it was fittin' to have a reception
committee, band and all. When Camden stepped out
onto the platform, the mayor asked, "How did you
like New York, Camden?"

"There was so much goin' on at the depot, I didn't get a chance to see the village."

Mad Dog

"Why are you so het up?"
"I had to shoot my dog."
"Was he mad?"
"Guess he weren't so darned pleased."

The Long Fezzle

My wife, Clara, died five o'clock this mornin'. It took half
the day to fix the box for her. I ran out of nails twice, bruised
my thumb with a hammer, and split three covers before I got
the fourth one nailed down tight. I pulled my back liftin'
Clara to the wagon, and the halter broke as we come out
of the barn, so we had to drive into town with Bessie pullin'
crooked.

Down the last hill, we got out of control, and Clara just slid off the back and shot straight through the post office window.

I ran in to see that no one was hurt and found Tut Tuttle, the postman, peerin' at me through the stamp window.
"Lucky I had the gratin' down," he said.
"Sure was," I replied.
"Did you see the preacher and the undertaker on the road?" he asked. "They started for your place an hour ago."

"Guess I missed them," I said. "I tell you, Tut," I said, "my day's been one long fezzle from beginnin' to end."

Aunt Mehitabel's Funeral

Aunt Mehitabel always said she was goin' to get out to
California before she died. Well, she just made it. She
wrote us that she had travelled there by way of Bangor
and that she did not like California because it was so far
from the ocean. She headed back East on the train and
got as far as Sacramento when she come down with the
coleramaubles and then the tizzik. The coleramaubles
will fell an ox, but it took the tizzik to drop Aunt
Mehitabel. She passed away on the train, and we wired
the stationmaster to crate her up and ship her back East.

When she arrived five days later, we rushed her through
the funeral service. It was the middle of August.
Then we got her out to the graveyard and was about
to lower her away when we pried up a board to have
a last look-see at the old girl. There inside was an admiral
in full dress uniform. Makin' the best of an unsettlin' situation,
we nailed the board back down, lowered the admiral, and
buried him quick in the hopes that somewhere Aunt
Mehitabel would be gettin' a twenty-one gun salute.

Virgil Bliss

Virgil Bliss was the dirtiest man in Hancock County.
Why, he was so dirty that in the wintertime, steam would
come out from between his sheets like it comes off a manure
pit. One summer people complained so much about Virgil
just bein' around, the constable brought him in before
Judge Dyer.

"Virgil, have you ever combed your hair?"
"Oh, I did once, but it almost killed me."
"How often do you change your shirt?"
"Oh, about once a year. Why? How often do you change yours?"
"Once a day and sometimes twice when it's hot."
"But judge, how can you call me dirty when you soil three hundred and sixty-five shirts to my one?"

Well, that was all the judge needed. His gavel come down and right then and there he sentenced Virgil to a bath.

It didn't take Virgil long to get dirty again. A month later Virgil was pullin' pots in the harbor when a pot pulled him instead. He sank straightaway to the bottom and never did come up.

People say the dirt just drug him down.

Acknowledgements

The characters of Bert and I and Virgil Bliss were first suggested by John Cochran. Nelson White told us "The Long Fezzle," and Charles Hester told us "Aunt Mehitabel's Funeral."

"Gagnon, World Champion Stove-Builder" is an adaptation of Ed Grant's finest story.

Alan Bemis, non-pareil New England storyteller, provided us with our initial inspiration and encouragement.